A SEARCH FOR JOY

Thoughts on

the Meaning of Faith

By Fae Malania

With Illustrations

By Muriel Wood

HALLMARK EDITIONS

A Search for Joy

THE MATTERHORN

I saw the Matterhorn once—just once, for a long moment.

We had come to Zermatt for a day or so, not to ski, just to see the mountain. After the scary cog railway and the walk through the hard and sounding snow we came into our room and I said, "Well, but where *is* it?"

"Right there," said my husband, pointing out the big window. But there was nothing there, only the snowy hills.

"It's the mist, you can't see it now. But it's there, rising over all the others."

"But there's no mist," I protested, amazed. "It's as clear as can be."

"That's how it looks to you," he answered, giving me a glance of loving concern. "But there *is* a mist, and the mountain is there."

"It must be awfully far away then."

"Oh no," he said, laughing a little. "Oh no, it's right there."

It is rude to be openly disbelieving of what other people hold to be true, so I said nothing more.

The next morning he was shaking me and laughing and called "Hurry up, wake up, it's there . . . "

I staggered to the window and while I was still saying, "But *it isn't*," it was. It didn't appear, it *was* there; it had always been there, beyond time, before space, close, alive, huge beyond any scale of comparison. Eternal silence, motionless power, being, perfect act. Presence.

I don't know how long I stood there, rapt, stunned, paralyzed, before that immense and ghostly reality. Then—I suppose the mist came back—I couldn't see it any more. But I knew now.

Sometimes people say, "But how can you really be *sure* God is there?" I can only laugh a little and say "Oh yes, He's there, He's right there."

A PIGEON

This morning there was a pigeon in the middle of East 36th Street who simply would not move, nor even glance up, as our car rolled murderously toward him. Just as I finally screamed, he contemptuously removed himself from under the wheels with the merest flick of a wing. My husband, who had remained calm throughout, remarked: " I can't teach him a thing about New York traffic that he doesn't know already. That's why he's so arrogant."

My husband has a great deal of empathy with animals. Once he told me about an encounter between a June bug and a spider. The drama, the suspense, the universality! Without moving from his chair [my husband] flew in the window, all wings and buzz and braggadocio, self-confident and stupid. Then, spiderlike, he marked his prey and placidly elbowed his way toward it, sinister but businesslike. Abruptly becoming himself, he scolded the foolish June bug back out the window, then turned on the spider and, in the strongest possible terms, denounced him. The nerve! Sneaking up on defenseless people like that behind their back! In this house the murder of one creature by another will simply not be tolerated! . . . Nettled, the spider withdrew to his lair to sulk.

"You mean," I said, after I had taken it all in, "you just *left* the spider there? If you wouldn't kill him you could at least have put him outside!"

"But he didn't want to be outside! The June bug came in by mistake, but the spider lives here. When a little fellow creature chooses to make his home with us, we should feel honored, and make him welcome."

"Well, then, if you're going to live with spiders, you have to get used to their killing June bugs. That's the way they are."

"You've missed the point," he said patiently. "Man is supposed to have dominion over all the animals. We're supposed to be in charge. That means if an animal chooses of his own free will to live with us—close to us, within our sphere of influence—he has to conform to our standards. That's the way the world is meant to be."

I wish I'd thought to say "The spiders, creeping after their prey, do seek their meat from God." But I didn't.

I still occasionally lower the moral tone of the universe by acts of hostility toward small fellow creatures who have sought the protection of our roof. But it troubles me a bit, it really does.

THE LIFE OF GOD

I took my coffee out to the porch this morning, putting on my glasses first in case a bird should drop by the birdbath. Instead, a butterfly floated onto the butterfly bush. I have deprived myself of butterflies, I thought sadly. All my life they've been dancing in the air, and I've had my nose stuck in a book. Even now, I'd be reading the New York *Times* except that it didn't come.

Beyond the butterfly bush is a holly tree, higher than the house. Roots, I thought. It has its roots in the earth. The earth holds it stable and straight and strong, the earth feeds it, rain comes to its roots through the earth.

Or is the natural life more like the visible part of the tree? Rooted and grounded secretly, it spreads

strong branches on the supporting air, answers sun and rain and wind, embraces in its large courtesy the other lives of birds and butterflies, squirrels and chipmunks and little bright-backed bugs.

Either or neither, or both. The whole tree lives by the life of God.

And I, planted to grow into a perfect nature, deep and tall and spreading, stunt my branches and wither my roots with malnutrition. In the midst of plenty, I'd rather read a book.

INDIANS

I don't remember the name of the town, or was it just a checkpoint, where we crossed from Canada into the Montana hills. We were just idling there in the car, thinking of nothing much, while the immigration man brooded over our mixed-up national affiliations. It was hot and bright and quiet, I felt lightheaded from days and days of beauty, my heart was all undefended.

In a split second, without a feather of warning, just the way it always used to happen, the Indians streaked out of nowhere and were upon us. Thundering hooves, lifting cloud of dust, high, bloodcurdling yells, knife-straight black hair swinging, eyes glittering like war fires—they were all around us, ringing us in, cutting off any hope of escape or rescue. There were about thirty of them, mostly about ten years old.

In all my years of Saturday afternoons in the balcony of the old Uptown, I never saw an Indian charge to match it.

We sat there frozen with incredulous joy while the immigration man laughed at our Eastern faces, though kindly. And the tribe swept unchecked across the border, exercising a lost sovereignty with undiminished style, restoring to the wide country its own and ancient name, conferring identity like a blessing by the superb authority of a known and natural presence.

Governments are often useful and often mean well, and must certainly be tolerated. But the land doesn't know them from Adam. So let them remember, from time to time, who's in charge here.

GLORIOUS GIFT OF LOVE

A spiritual writer I've been reading lately informs me that I ought to love God because it is only due to His great goodness that He does not annihilate me right this minute. This gives me a rather vivid insight into the emotions of the Negro who is urged to love all us good kind white liberals. I don't think the comparison is quite so unapt as it may seem, either. I will stick my neck out and say that the question of justice does exist between creator and creature, as well as between man and man.

He also says that, if it is the sacred duty of the child to love its father, how much more are we obliged, etc. etc. Not a word about the duty of the father to love the child.

This is the sort of thing that gives religion a bad name. If we are going to be anthropomorphic (and, as far as I am concerned, we are), why can't we choose the more likable aspects of our human nature to measure God by? Why not assume that He is, at the very least, as good as we would like to be if only we had a little better control over our impulses? We would not, for instance, think about annihilating our child and then decide, graciously and capriciously, not to. We would give him, if we knew how, an oceanic love, joyous, without limit or regret, without afterthoughts or recriminations; and at the same time, a watchful, caring discipline, individually tailored to the child—not to scare him out of his dear little wits but to equip him with a clear-sighted knowledge of the things that belong to his peace, and the moral force and freedom to live by them.

We would not announce that it was his duty to love us. We would say, as a simple matter of fact, that he loves us because we first loved him.

I'm not sure, wicked as I am, that gratitude is the most reliable motive for love. But if God gives us grace to be grateful, let us be grateful not just because He lets us live. So does the government. Let us be grateful for the free, uncost-counting, inalienable, lavish, glorious gift of love.

ON MY DINING ROOM TABLE

On my dining room table, at the moment, is the magazine section of the New York *Post* from two days ago; half the Long Island paper of the same date; my kitchen timer, put there this morning so I'd know when the eggs were done; my dark glasses; the top of a box I brought home from the bakery yesterday; a pretty little three-minute timer which I used a few minutes ago to take my temperature by (it was normal); today's mail, unopened; this week's *Life*; my checkbook; a checkbook filler; a letter from my mother; a note I wrote to my son three days ago when I left the house; a note he wrote to me the same day when *he* left the house; a cup of coffee, half full; a pencil; a swatch of fabric representing the sofa slipcover before last; the purse I was carrying yesterday, wide open; an empty gray paper bag from a bookstore; a pliofilm wrapper for a pair of white kid gloves which I wore last Thursday; an emery board; two green stamps; a bottle of pills; two foil packets of hand lotion; four flyers from a department store, advertising things I may decide to buy; a pocket edition of the Psalms, KJV; and an album of children's records which I mean to give away, as we're all grown up now.

Also on the same table, the notebook in which I write and my two elbows, supporting the hands that hold my head. What am I to make of all this? (I just took my temperature again and it's still normal, there must be something wrong with that thermometer.)

I know the solution in principle, of course. Pick up any one of these objects, and put it wherever it belongs, and then go on to the next, and so on. On a better day I suppose I could have the table clear in about ninety seconds, or three television commercials. But if this were a better day I wouldn't be telling you all this. Today, I can't. I don't *know* why, that's what I'm trying to explain!

My hand barely begins to reach out toward, for instance, the old newspapers. In a hideous, shivering instant I see everything on the table not as separable, manageable things over which even I might establish dominion, but as a mass, an indivisible glob of things, a surly, lifeless mob of things, a whole more incoherent than the sum of its parts. (God is Three-in-One, but the Devil's name is Legion.)

The brain-to-hand impulse is struck dead, as if by a jealous god.

I turn away and pace (you've seen tigers) to and fro in the house, walking up and down in it. The vacuum cleaner is in the middle of the living room floor. I pause, I could use it or I could put it away; but my mind is not in communication with my hand. I wheel about, my feet take me to the kitchen, where the breakfast dishes are in the sink. I cannot decide to do them, I turn again. The beds are unmade but I swing away, back to the dining room table, to the kitchen, to and fro, up and down. I am very tired, but my unconscious mind is in communication with my legs and I cannot stop. I sit down and then, without knowing how it happens, I am on my feet again, walking.

Do you see? I cannot clear the table, I cannot wash the dishes, which should I do first? Don't you see, I cannot begin. I cannot *choose* to begin.

Oh how will I ever explain this to you? Let me try another way.

Over and over I have read and repeated and thought about and clung to and yearned over those words, "All my fresh springs are in Thee." Water, think of it, clear, sparkling, lively, springing up fresh and pure from its source deep in the earth. So all meaningful action springs from a hidden, uncorrupt source.

The mind that chooses, that forms the thought, Let *this* be done *now*, is like the mind that formed the world. Let There Be Light: and Chaos, which was not, began to be filled with all that was. There would be another day for the next step, a separate motion within the mind of God for the moon and the stars, the green herb, the beasts of the field. The mind which decides and orders and instigates has its deep springs in the mind of God.

The hand that reaches out, with knowledge and power, to pick up an old newspaper from a welter of odds and ends, is an image of the hand of God. It has authority because it moves, however unknowingly, under the authority of God.

What, then, if the mind cannot choose and the hand is blind, knowing nothing, moving without power or purpose? Chaos is come again.

Chaos is nothing; is Satan. Separate objects on a table are an unintelligible jumble, because the principle of individuation is not in him. The mind cannot differentiate and choose, because in him is no order. The hand can only move blindly in the air, because he does not make, or renew, or restore, or keep, or hold. The feet can only devour the earth, because in him is neither destination nor rest.

From the spring of nothing, nothing will flow.

God, Thou God of the living and not of the dead, send my roots rain.

EDEN IN NAZARETH

There is a story that Jesus, when He was a child, played at making birds out of clay, and when He tossed them into the air, they flew. Well, I don't believe that. There is another version of His childhood that I believe even less: that sob story about the despised carpenter's family, outcast, poor, hungry, cold, and sad. Nobody despises carpenters nowadays, and I'm sure they didn't then, either, not in that little peasant backwater. There may have been a famine, of course, there so often was; but if everyone else was eating, I think the Holy Family was, too.

I have a different idea of what it must have been like in that Holy Household. He didn't make birds, but He first, since Adam, named them.

Imagine what it was like watching Him grow, seeing His infant eyes first discover a bird and, in delighted recognition, know its nature. What a blazing light of reality must have grown in that House as His world widened, as He saw and touched and handled the common things of the visible world. How the fire must have leapt, how the wood of the table must have shone in the sunlight, how water must have sparkled in the pail, how stone and earth must have described geology. And the flowers beside the door, the wild flowers beyond, the fig tree, the olive, the vine, with what a light they must have burned when the light of His eyes touched them. How the birds must have sung, and the cat purred, and the lambs played. Goats, too, rabbits, butterflies, caterpillars, field mice, little lizards and garden snakes, the ox and the ass, the hen with her chicks, all struck with the lightning of His glance, their natures known and revealed.

How the hearts of Mary and Joseph must have sung, to see the unchanged world in its changed beauty, seeing as He saw.

Those were the hidden years, one with the earth's sweet being in the beginning, Eden in Nazareth. Then He was daily God's delight, rejoicing always before Him.

MY GREAT-GRANDMOTHER

Pondering on the nature of contemplation, I have been led to think of my great-grandmother. I don't remember what she looked like, I have never seen a picture of her, I don't remember anyone ever telling me anything about her; and she died, so far as I am concerned, before history began. But I remember her.

I was two (that was the year we went Back Home to visit, so it must have been then). There is nothing at all to say who the woman in my memory picture was—why couldn't she have been just any woman standing in a doorway? But I know.

I was outside the door, on the porch, looking way up at her from my 33 inches or so. She was inside, looking down at me, her right hand crossed over in front of her holding the screen door. She couldn't, of course, really have been holding it. In a Southern Illinois summer with a temperature of 108° in the

shade and flies and mosquitoes as yet unacquainted with insecticide, nobody held open screen doors. Either I had just gone out and she was closing it, or I wanted to come in and she was opening it. Or maybe she had just given me a cup of cold water from the pump at the kitchen sink. The door was about at midpoint, but I was looking up at her through the screen, not the opening.

It could have lasted no more than a flash of time (otherwise the flies would have got in), but my great-grandmother and I have had all the rest of my life to share this moment, to taste its quality, to assay its meaning. It is still in my mind, perfect, mysterious, unfathomed.

I was looking at her face, through the screen, but I don't remember her face. I remember her presence, and a deep, still happiness to be in her presence. I remember the expansion of time, like a slowing of breath, so there was nothing else I had to do but look at her, and grow in the warmth of her sun. There was all the time in the world or there was no time at all any more. I was trusting and at peace, quite safe. I was entirely myself, simple in substance, of single eye, but peacefully aware of an infinite capacity.

If a moment of true communion with an ordinary, no doubt flawed, human being could be so much to me—a garden enclosed, a stilling of time and temporalities, a flowering of happiness, an intuition of infinite possibility, a secret never forgotten, never fully read. . . . If all this can be and remain in a moment of human communion, what must it be like to see for an instant the face of God in the shadows, behind the screen? To stand in His presence in still and motionless joy, and know the warmth and shining of His sun?

I keep all these things and ponder them in my heart.

PROPHET, POTTAGE, AND LION'S DEN

God's idea of what is suitable for us—or even possible—so rarely coincides with ours.

Take Habbakuk. There he was, starting out with a hot dinner for the field hands, when suddenly the Angel of the Lord happened along and told him to carry it to Babylon, where Daniel was in a lion's den. And, I suppose, hungry.

Listen, said Habbakuk, who though a prophet was a reasonable man, I've never even been to Babylon. How on earth am I supposed to find it, let alone find a particular lion's den in it, let alone serve this stew piping hot after I get there?

The Angel, not deigning to reply, just grabbed him by the hair of his head and "through the vehemency of his spirit" set him down in Babylon, in the lion's den. (And Daniel, though pleased, does not appear to have been much surprised.)

Prophet and pottage and lion's den seem a bit remote. But the absurdity of the demand and the vehemency of the spirit—how familiar. The scalp hurts, in memory and anticipation.

GOD ENJOYS THE HYENA

The animal kingdom holds for us such an infinite variety of delights: beauty, majesty, delicacy, comedy, gaiety, strength, speed, song, grace, grandeur. What a God, to think of such forms to create, such ways of life to set in motion!

But mosquitoes seem unnecessary; buzzards are, to the merely human eye, unattractive; the ferocity of the wolverine lacks the burning-brightness of the tiger. It's the hyena, though, that gives me pause. A more depraved looking animal cannot be imagined. The very sight of him is really nauseating.

But since he is an animal, he cannot be depraved. It is a fault of vision in me that sees that sneaky, ungainly body, those cold intrusive eyes, those hideous, loose jaws, as evil.

God didn't simply install the hyena as you would plumbing, to take care of a sanitation problem. He made him. Given what I say I believe of the nature of God, I am absolutely required to believe that He made the hyena with pleasure, looked upon him with love, and saw that he was good. God *enjoys* the hyena, just as if he were a meadowlark.

It's thoughts like this that make me realize how little I have yet understood of God.

† *NOVEMBER 22, 1963* †

All his bright light gone from the world. What can I say, even these many months later, about a death—a life—so numinous? So sun-bright with a truth that darkens the eyes, so formidable with meaning darkly sensed?

What was it we saw in him? Why did we weep so? Why do we still file past that grave in a long, unending line, half in homage, half in a kind of search? What was in him that only our grief told us we had known?

He was the President, and he cared about this country the way we want a President to care; more, he cared about the world the way the world wants a President to care. He thought greatness was possible and was prepared, quite courteously, to insist on it. He thought that meant goodness, too. He was gay and visibly brave, pleasing to look at and fun to

listen to. He loved his children, he made us laugh. He died young and, it seemed to us, senselessly. Who could help weeping, all his bright light gone from the world?

But these are details. What we saw in him, behind the accidental splendor of his capacities and accomplishments and personal beguilement, was our own human nature in its splendid, ordinary truth. He swam through flaming seas with a wounded shipmate; but he did it simply, as we might put out a casual hand to save a companion from falling. He made terrifying decisions, for all of us and all the future; but simply and seriously, as we might do our plain best to find the right turn of the road if the wheel were in our hands. Life showered him with gifts and stormed him with blows, opened up to him possibilities and fenced him in with denials, dealt out joy and pain with evenhanded lavishness; and through it all he walked in the glorious liberty of the children of God, enslaved to nothing, refusing nothing, freely choosing to be what he was, to do what was to be done, to bear what was to be borne, fully and strongly engaged in the exercise of all his powers along lines of excellence.

Sun, moon, and star, being bright, and sent to do their office, are obedient. Man, being bright with a greater light and sent to do a higher office, isn't always. But he was; more than most. In his obedience, he shed about him the true and ordinary human light, the unique image, that is ours alone in all creation, of Light itself; and we were willing for a season to rejoice in his light.

But he was not the first to show us how bright our light might be. There are others, there will be others still, brothers and teachers. Let us begin then, obedient to our office, to study from them how to shine.

THE HABIT OF RECOLLECTION

The only thing you can hope to carry home from a retreat is the habit of recollection, the practice of the presence of God.

The beauty of choir and candles is not exportable, religious emotions don't keep. Devotional practices, no matter how sweet, are ashes in the mouth when they interfere with duty. You may snatch an hour of solitude, but the cat will not observe silence. The meditations and reflections of yesterday, filled with light and joy and strength, were, however, yesterday. Today is today.

In the end the only thing left is God, and God will not be domesticated. You can't build a framework strong enough to hold Him.

He is here and now. His voice invites us now, and He is waiting every moment for us to respond.

The trouble is, we're usually back in the middle of last week, poking around under old stones and thinking, where *can* He have gotten to?

WHAT SHE HAD BEEN GIVEN

I read once a very spirited defense of St. Thérèse of Lisieux against the awful charge of being neurotic. What the author was really saying, with considerable heat, was that it was irreverent to suppose that God would perform His mighty works in the souls of inferior people like neurotics. Well.

Let us consider the bare bones of her life: her birth to a mother already fatally ill; the early loss of her mother; the intensity and yet the odd staginess of her relation to her father; that curious childhood breakdown; her lifelong, hungry search for a mother and the shattering loss of one mother figure after another; her "baby of the family" ways and the long agony of self-discipline with which she broke the ties—hands clinging for dear life to the stair rail to keep from throwing away all her gains and flinging herself, again, into the bondage of her human needs.

All this any neurotic can recognize. To say it is normal is to make nonsense of the word "normal" —which anyway *is* nonsense, maybe, but that's not the point. The damage to her personality was done, and cannot be denied. It could not have been her fault. It could never be erased. It did not make her inferior any more than it made her a saint. It was morally neutral, neither good nor bad. It was, simply, what she had been given to live with. *How* she lived with it, and around it and over it and in spite of it and through it, was what made her a saint.

With the same background and emotional equipment she might have become a weepy clinging vine, and everyone would have said, "Oh Thérèse Martin! She's just a neurotic."

God does not allow defective and damaged minds and hearts to be, and then turn up His nose at them in comfortable superiority, as we do. He gives to *each* human being—and this means the neurotic, the mad, the subnormal—the capacity to be a saint: that is, to fill his vessel full of holiness, here in this life, no matter what sort of odd size or shape that vessel may be.

The saints we know by that name are a very few of the many, each of them a burning and a shining light to illuminate for us some particular facet of holiness. It may be rare for the subnormal to achieve a kind of sanctity from which the rest of us can learn, but I gather that it has been done. The mad are seldom able to live a life that we can make sense of as a model; though, even here, I suspect biographical suppressions or misunderstandings in the lives of a few of the saints. But for the neurotic there is no such difficulty—quite the opposite. If he does become a saint, the flaw in his character will condition his sanctity, shape it, give it its characteristic color and flash; and may make it of particular value to us as a model, since—come now, we're not all that normal, are we?

But whether Saints of the Church or secret saints or struggling sinners, never mind. Do we really know how many graces come to us from the patient endurance of the mentally deficient who can't even be taught to pray? How much may depend on the bare intent of a soul toward God through one more nightmare hallucination? Can we even guess how the Cross is carried behind those terrible and impenetrable veils?

I hope when we have finally brought ourselves to understand that Negroes are full members of the human race and as much entitled to ordinary respect as anybody else, we'll turn our attention next to those who are "different" more than just skin deep.

OF BEING A PERFECTIONIST

Psychiatrists, teachers, friends, relatives, and other experts have been accusing me for years of being a perfectionist. I don't mean they are so blind as to think I don't need improving; but my standards, they keep telling me, are absurd. Do I, for heaven's sake, expect myself to be perfect? Who do I think I am, anyway?

At this point the conversation goes to pieces, because we're not talking about the same thing. The theory is clear—I am not perfect, and too much self-reproach over this obvious fact has more to do with pride than with humility. But practice—now that is another matter. At what point may I excuse myself from further effort and say "I've done all I could, after all I'm not perfect"? This is a practical question and I'd like, if you please, a practical answer.

"I'm so tired I can't do another thing . . . I cannot stand this for one more minute . . . I have been as patient as anyone possibly could . . . I have tried as hard as anybody could be expected to. . . ." None of these statements quite rings true, does it? One more step, ten seconds more of patience, another instant of endurance, another ounce of effort—who can say this is impossible? Who can say it wouldn't make a difference?

It seems to me, if I'm lying on my deathbed entirely paralyzed except for one finger, and the cat comes up and wants his chin scratched, I'm supposed to scratch it. I don't say I would, or that very many other people would either, but let's not cloud the issue with slighting remarks about perfectionism.

The subject of this discussion is charity and grace.

Charity requires me to lift the last movable finger and God will certainly give me the grace to do it, if I ask Him nicely. Of course if a friend holds my hand or a scandalized nurse removes the cat, I am thus excused. But I can't just lie there and say I don't feel like it. Who do I think I am, anyway, to deny the universe the full measure of my charity just because I'm dying? (or exasperated? or in a hurry? or because some scoundrel has treated me less well than I think I deserve?)

Still, we do deny it, you and I and all our friends and relations. Dr. Zhivago said he was dying of lies. I wonder if we're not all languishing away, like genteel Victorian ladies, of anemic imperfectionism.

DON'T PANIC

Standing as I do at the very epicenter of an entrenched and long-established disorder, where shall I put my finger first to say, Let a new life begin? "Don't panic," my husband says, "Remember, God created the whole world in only six days, and He didn't panic."

Mary Ellen Chase says we have lost our sense of enduring values—beauty and quiet, discipline and work. Everyone is always saying things like that,

and I always nod solemnly and decide to reform my life. But she said *exactly* that, and so illumined the whole subject that I am really almost persuaded that I will.

It is the order she put them in that is so enlightening. The world is full of women who work far more dutifully and effectively than I do, and if there is a woman less disciplined, I don't see how she gets by at all. Why then are these admirable ladies no closer than I am to "enduring values" (and I don't really think they are)? Because they've got the order wrong.

Beauty first—and no fly-by-night witchery, but the kind that can't exist without the rest of the list. A work of art is created in the quiet of a mind disciplined, concentrated, drawn in to its center (even if in no other way is the artist disciplined at all); and with hard labor. The practice of a craft, too, is work, requires discipline, and quiet attention, and results in beauty. A house cannot be kept in such relative beauty as is possible for it without quiet, a discipline, and work (if God had set the stars in their courses and then gone off and left them, the universe would have been hopelessly snarled five minutes after Creation, as every housewife knows). The work of training a family life into ways (disciplines) of beauty can be done, if at all, only with a quiet spirit.

To allow a human soul to develop into anything resembling beauty takes an ocean of interior silence, a large spiritual room to turn around in. Quiet for thought to form, and moral choice; for loving contemplation of other people; for contemplative weighing of how each day is spent. Quiet of the many voices of the self until the will is, in St. John of the Cross's words, "free, solitary and pure." How much discipline and work this must take!

But quiet, if it comes first, is a usurper. The perfect silence of the state prison, maintained by excellent discipline and hard work, does not give rise to enduring value.

Discipline, too, can be a lovely thing—the free and rational choice of means in the light of ends clearly known; an intricate simplicity in which nothing is wasted or scattered or scamped. But to what end? Ants are disciplined, but beauty does not result. (Nor, I should imagine, does quiet. Just the tread of all those marching feet must be deafening, to an ant.)

And work alone? Without the shaping of discipline . . . without the repose of silence for the soul or the body . . . neither creating beauty nor keeping it? So must they work in Hell.

Beauty and quiet, discipline and work. For the creation of a world or the conversion of a life, here is a fourfold, single Rule, a little Rule for beginners, containing in it nothing harsh or burdensome to be borne, though a certain strictness may result. And, to further paraphrase St. Benedict, the workshop in which we may diligently practice it is the enclosure of daily circumstance, and stability in all those daily paths which God has prepared for us to walk in.

CHILDREN

Some of my best friends, like St. Francis de Sales and St. Thérèse of Lisieux, are always going on about the perfection of love and trust to be found in children— the simplicity of the little child who, holding his father's hand, knows he is safe—the effortless goodness of the child who looks to his mother's smile to tell him he is right, and never doubts what he sees in her face.

How can they say such things?

Childhood has always seemed to me a long night of confused shapes and uncertain ground, darkness streaked by nightmare, the devil as a lion seeking whom he may devour, destruction wasting in the noonday. An extreme view, but so is theirs. I think modern psychology leans in my direction.

They talk, these saints, about being with God like a child who, held in his mother's arms, can only babble over and over again "I love you." But I remember the exact sound of the voice of a little boy, held in an angry mother's arms, who could only babble—howl, rather—"Mother dear, I love you. I *love* you, Mother *dear!*'' This incident, seen thirty years ago when I was already not quite a child, has never left my mind.

Still, how can I dismiss all this *gemutlichkeit* as an amiable lack of scientific observation on the part of unworldly priests and nuns? After all, it's Gospel. ''Except ye become as little children. . . .'' He must have meant something.

And I think now I have a clue.

I've been reading about Maria Montessori and what she says are the normal characteristics of the child, the essential personality that is revealed when

the conditions of his life are right for him (as in the ordinary course of things they certainly are not).

This "normal" child has an innate love of silence, and a deep delight in attending to the small, living sounds of silence, to the still voice that whispers out of it. He has a love of order and a strong and peaceful will to participate in its creation and preservation. He is open to direction, self-disciplined because he must be to get at the good he sees, cooperative because nothing pinches him. He lives at ease with time, redeeming the moments without haste or anxiety. He has a vigorous and searching intellect which examines, sorts, orders, names, combines, constructs; and is refreshed rather than fatigued by its labors. He works meditatively, seeing the object of his attention with his eyes, handling it with his hands, walking all around it in fact and in spirit, considering it, learning its nature, and from it forming his own. He uses all the materials of his kinetic, sensory, emotional, intellectual, spiritual world in one undivided process of "creating his character." The chief of his ways is joy.

Montessori says there is a "sensitive period" for every phase of learning—what isn't learned at the right time is irrecoverable. At eighteen or so, she says, development stops. After that, the individual just gets older.

Well, maybe. But Jesus does seem to be saying,

doesn't He, that we can become as little children?

I mean to find out how.

FACES

There is a rather odd experience I have every once in a while. At night, when I am almost asleep but not quite, I see faces. Hundreds and hundreds of them—or so it seems—in quick succession, caught in a particular expression, laughing, puzzled, angry, troubled, speaking, listening, sorrowing, brooding, just turning away, just now looking up—a million poses, a million faces, never any two alike. So many, I had not thought death had undone so many.

It has occurred to me, belatedly, that these are real faces. Even a great artist can't invent one. He can alter the set of his model's eyes, borrow a bit of his own psychic structure for an expression, add this and subtract that. But to think up a face, starting from scratch, is beyond him. And, of course, beyond me.

So. The faces I see are real. Either people I've actually seen, in life, or people who exist (or have existed, or will exist?) and of whom I have some extrasensory knowledge. In the absence of evidence let us assume the simpler and more probable hypothesis.

Walking along all the streets of all the cities of

my life, all the days of my life, my mind as usual squirreling along in its own tiny absorptions, some faculty in me has been recording with vigilant accuracy every human face my eye has lit upon.

The other day, walking along 42nd Street, I saw the faces that passed for the first time with this same faculty of total vision. They flared in my eyes like lightning, each one a unique culmination of all history, an incalculable dimension of reality, a mystery clothing the miracle of Person. While I was still eclipsed in wonder at one, another came, and another, there was no time to absorb the successive shocks. At the end of a crosstown block I was dizzy with perception, exhausted, almost sick; as I always am from the night visions.

My husband, who has never had the night visions and did not at first understand what I meant about them, has seen the faces in clear daylight for years. But he is not exhausted, he is exhilarated. When he feels depressed he goes out and walks the crowded streets, soaking up faces like a sponge, till the marvel of Adam restores him to joy.

It was only the other day that we began to understand each other, to see that we were both describing the same experience. What still remains to be discovered is why we respond to it so differently.

Perhaps I am not quite ready to share the world with so many sovereign identities, so many new-minted images of the King. I'm not quite willing—quite yet—to see them. And so, I am compelled to suffer them.

GOD'S EXTRAVAGANT BLESSING

I hate to be out when it's just getting dark. The minute the first lamp goes on, with me on the outside looking in, a polar icecap descends over my soul. I am convinced that I no longer have a home, I'm doomed to wander forever in chill shadows outside the circle of other people's lamplight. (I am an indifferent housekeeper, but a truly devoted homekeeper.)

The other evening after a storm of Christmas shopping, I came slinking home to a dark house at five o'clock on a winter afternoon, my psychic balance out of whack as it always is on these occasions. The house was empty, hollow, unhuman, sullen with silence.

I love silence—I'm always saying so—but sometimes it can be an absence of footsteps, a muteness of voices, a lack of music. I love solitude, but sometimes it can be an absence of faces, a want of living hands and loving eyes.

I switched on all the lights, turned up the furnace, put some Christmas songs (voices) on the gramophone, picked up the cat (purrs) and just sat and shivered, yearning for my two men to walk in the door and make life start again.

"It seemed so cold when I got home this evening," I exclaimed about 11:30 that night. "You've said that five times since dinner," my husband replied kindly. "You've gotten the information across very well indeed. Now what exactly are you trying to convey by it?"

What I'm trying to convey, I suppose, is how good and joyful a thing it is to dwell together in unity. Like precious oil poured out, sluiced out, spilled over, and running in rivers. Like dew falling on the holy hills. God's extravagant blessing and promise of life forevermore.

THE QUANTITY OF A HAZEL NUT

I had an awful dream once, it was a terrible dream, terrible things happened in it. There wasn't any future in my dream. It was all gone, lost, irretrievable; and by my fault, by my own fault.

At the deepest point of my despair, in the twinkling of an eye—though nothing was changed—everything was changed. I was holding—something—in the curve of my palm. Its weight was good to the hand, it was very solid, round. It might have been an apple, or a globe. It was all that mattered, and in it was everything. Even in my sleep, I think I cried for joy.

A long time later, in the Revelations of Dame Julian of Norwich, a fourteenth-century English anchoress, I met my dream again, and I knew it at once.

"In this," she says (this vision or, as she always calls it, shewing)—"In this He shewed me a little thing, the quantity of a hazel nut, lying in the palm of my hand, and to my understanding it was as round as any ball. I looked thereupon and thought: 'What may this be?' And I was answered in a general way, thus: 'It is all that is made.' I marvelled how it could last, for methought it might fall suddenly to naught for littleness. And I was answered in my understanding: 'It lasts and ever shall last because God loves it, and so hath all-thing its being through the love of God.' "

A TENDENCY TO ANSWER BACK

This is the day which the Lord hath made:
            we will rejoice and be glad in it.
I try to make a practice of saying this verse as soon as I wake up, to remind me. Only I have a tendency to answer back. Like "I wouldn't mind rejoicing so much if they'd just let me stay in bed." Or—this

morning—"Rejoice and be glad in *this*, what are they talking about?" (Note how the old gods linger, in that "They"—or the Fates or the Furies, or whoever they are.)

It was raining this morning. Well, not just raining. It was trying, with a sort of dull, mindless determination, to blot out the world once and for all. It's still raining. All last night, all day today, where will it end—a steady, meaningless, uninterrupted, unvarying, uninflected *drench*, as if automation had now turned up in nature, to throw individual raindrops out of work.

Rejoice? Oh I just hate it!

However, let's see now. There's been a drought, and I do care about the food supply, don't I, and the farmers, and the reservoirs? But the farms are mostly in the next county, and the reservoirs are upstate, so why doesn't the rain. . . ? Then can't I summon up a fellow creaturely feeling for the thirsty blades of grass in my own front lawn? Yes but after all, it rained all night!

I'll never get anywhere like this, trying to aim a theoretical good will at the crops in order to avoid thinking about the rain. What I have to rejoice in—to love and be glad in—is, exactly, the rain. Because the Lord hath made it, and there it is.

O ye Heavens, bless ye the Lord. O ye Waters, O ye Showers, O ye Winds of God, bless ye the Lord.

Praise him and magnify him forever. Is *that* what it's doing? Why, yes. I'm the one who's out of tune. My song of praise is full of footnotes claiming exemptions.

This is the world which the Lord hath made, and all His works bless Him at every heartbeat of creation, just by being. In the interest of accuracy, I must at least learn to see straight.

When I can see what is really there, as it is in very Truth, as His hands made it and His eyes see it, then —ah, then! Love will come singing, rejoicing and being glad.

GO WITHOUT!

It is true that the voice of God, when we hear it, speaks in the very cadence of our own voice, the very idiom of our own mind. But I don't regard that as cause for suspicion. I can't see why God shouldn't be perfectly at home in the subconscious.

His remarks to me tend to be pretty short and snappy. They usually depress my pretensions, as Jane Austen might have put it; they often make me laugh; and they always—this, really, is why I believe they're authentic messages—they always cheer me up and stiffen my spine. Temporarily, because of my sins, but every little bit helps.

Or sometimes it's a saint conveying the message. For instance: Walking out of my room one difficult, disorganized day, on my way downstairs to a confusion of duties I didn't feel up to coping with, my eye lit on St. Thérèse.

"Help!" I exclaimed, without ceremony. And she: "Go without."

I was really taken aback. And yet it was so like her—so exactly what she would say. I went on downstairs laughing, and got through it all somehow. So, she answered, and refused, and the refusal was all the help I needed. Just the sort of paradox Heaven seems to delight in.

Once, though, God made me a speech so long and so much in my own characteristic vein of sarcasm that I would certainly have doubted it very much if it hadn't been so telling. In church one Sunday morning the priest turned from the altar and said—Christ said, through the priest—"Come unto me all ye that travail and are heavy laden, and I will refresh you." "Will you indeed!" I murmured, with a sad, sardonic glance up at the crucifix. The answer almost knocked me flat. "What do *you* want with refreshment? I thought you were supposed to be so interested in intercession."

By the time I had recovered from this unsettling encounter we were clear through the consecration and praying that we might worthily receive His most precious Body and Blood, be filled with His grace and heavenly benediction and made one body with Him that He might dwell in us, and we in Him.

So I went to the altar rail and received, with maybe just a shade less ingratitude than usual, the solid food by which I live. I am nourished, I thought. All that my soul needs to feed muscle and sinew, to build blood and bone, is provided. But the delights of taste, the pleasure of hunger satisfied, the well-being of vitality restored—suppose all this is passed along, through me, to someone else?

I have enough. How petty, to begrudge an alms for the poor!

THE CAMEL

Until *Lawrence of Arabia* I had never actually seen a camel.

Of course I've seen plenty of them processing across Christmas cards, standing around on cigarette packages, sulking in zoos despising their surroundings. The way they look is both laughable and unsympathetic, and suggests that they don't know how to enjoy themselves.

And I've read about them. They are morose, disagreeable, and unloving. They bite their masters. They have neither the generosity to make the best of their lot nor the spirit to put up a really good fight against it. Spiritually speaking, the camel is a total loss.

He is, in fact, a disconcerting reminder of that chilling old theory that God made the world and everything in it for the use of man, and for nothing else whatever. Could God have done such an awful thing? Could He have breathed life into even one creature who is—in himself, for himself—just nothing at all? Created a conscious being to live a life of joyless utility, to be a tool, a convenience, an object? It doesn't bear thinking about.

But now I've really seen a camel.

I've heard one, too—in fact, a whole caravan of them. In the morning when the camp begins to wake, they lift up their voices and greet the day, groaning, bellowing, yawping one after another until the desert roars with a glorious, blaring cacophony. Maybe it's complaint, but there's nothing mean or petty about it. I wouldn't be surprised if that's what brought down the walls of Jericho.

But to really see the camel, you have to see him running. When he walks, lurching and swaying, rolling and pitching, you would think each muscle was headed in a different direction. When he begins to run he's like one of those heavy, ungainly birds who can hardly get off the ground—but when they do, they own the whole wide sky.

Given time enough and desert enough, he manages to get his ramshackle collection of bones all moving together, he picks up speed, stretches out longer and longer, and then . . . now, there is a *camel*! At full gallop, his neck way out ahead of him, his whole fantastic shape a bewilderment of undulations, fast, powerful, free as a desert storm, he's wild and weird and gorgeous beyond belief, an authentic aboriginal marvel. The whole wide ocean of sand is his; he owns it.

Compared to the camel, the horse is an over-simplification.

Who would ask of such a lord of life that he also cultivate an amiable personality?

BOLD AS BRASS

One thing that cheers me enormously is the barefaced confidence with which St. Peter says, "Lord, thou knowest that I love thee," even though not many days ago he has denied him thrice.

You'd think he might have curled up in a damp ball, moaning, "Oh I've really ruined everything this time . . . what will he think of me . . . it's all very well to say I'll never do it again, but why should he believe that . . . oh no I'll never be able to look him in the eye again. . . ."

But not St. Peter. With true apostolic verve, he bounced right back. Bold as brass he made his claim, counting not on his own proven weakness but on the character of his Lord, whom now, at last, he knew.

On those days when everything I touch turns to guilt and gloom and my heart lies limp as a fish within me, I think of St. Peter and mutter stubbornly, "Lord thou knowest that I love thee."

I'm not so sure, myself, but Lord, thou knowest.

A SIGN

A small miracle has been taking place right under my nose for years, and I've never even thought about it.

A little plaque of St. Anthony, with the words (in Italian) "Protect our house," has been resting in a rather transient and unregarded way on a ledge in the kitchen for nearly as long as I can remember. An orphanage in Sicily sent it to us in return for a contribution, and since it had already been blessed I couldn't throw it away, so there it stayed, right where it lit.

The miracle is, though everything else in the house collects its weight in dust every day or so, this doesn't. There it stands, pinkly plastic, surrounded by gas fumes, flying grease, and spilling liquids (we

are a rather ham-handed family), and for weeks at a time I never go near it. But when it finally occurs to me to wash it, it's clean as a whistle.

St. Anthony was never a favorite of mine, either. I suppose it's nice of him, in a way, to find things for people; but to tell the truth, it seems a bit trivial. Once in a while, when somebody is really distressed over losing something, all right. But when he constantly allows himself to be so employed, I should think he might spend his whole heaven locating the other glove, and nobody would be a bit the better for it.

Still, how odd, this immunity from household hazard. Can it be a sign, meant for my instruction? Could it be that a saint who appears to me to be wasting his time is in fact doing just what God asks of him?

THE WHOLE CHURCH

A saintly priest composed a very short morning prayer for busy people, the first third of which is, O God, I love you. I could never say that. Spontaneously, of course, if it flew from my heart to my lips without a pause. But not deliberately, with forethought.

What I can say is, Lord thou knowest that I love

thee. This phrase, carrying its heavy freight of association, brings the whole church swinging into its wake. It contains within it the defection of St. Peter, the fiery confirmation of Pentecost, the martyrdom of the Apostles. It says that my love is firmly grounded in His, fragile and fidgety though it may seem. And other things it says, some that I know now and more that I hope to know hereafter.

But—O God, I love you. So flat, so bare, and . . . is it *really* true? It embarrasses me.

The same priest once asked an unbelieving young man to say daily a prayer which began something like this: O God, if there is a God. . . . The young man later said that he tried it for a while, but then he began to perceive very faintly the outline of something real behind it; and he didn't like it.

We can't be sure, of course, at this distance, exactly what it was he didn't like. But it does spring to the eye—or ear—that this is no way to talk to God, once you begin to have an uneasy notion that He exists. You don't say "there is a God" in that offhand, inventorying manner, standing in the awesome presence of Him Who Is.

But there *are* words for this: Lord, I believe; help thou mine unbelief. If the seeker is unable to say the first phrase, the second alone will do. He may say, Help thou mine unbelief, times without number and it may mean nothing to him. But if it begins to show itself a door opening, it will not open directly onto a gangplank. Behind that door is Christ.

Our words, issuing from such a dark and unknown continent within, are full of unsuspected snares, hidden windings to confound the unwary, bottomless pits lightly camouflaged with pretty leafage. They are paths which may at any turn of the way end in a blank wall.

The church's words are paths where we may walk at liberty, in delight and in safety. When we set our feet in them, there is no place to go but to God.

SEARCH OUT JOY

Most of us, in spite of pleasant circumstances and fun and games, lead lives of quiet desperation. Sometimes we hardly even notice it, supported as we are by a thick web of human relationships, shored up by a multiplicity of small pleasures. Other times it's all we can do to scratch together a few emotional odds and ends to try to draw a decent veil over the face of reality.

We'd do better to turn and go after it, instead.

To begin with, never mind pleasure. Search out joy. Pleasure is its shadow, with no more substance than a shadow. But joy is real, a secret splendor running through all creation.

Like gold, it doesn't lie about the streets waiting to be picked up. It has to be dug for, with diligence and passion. It's in people, to be found through the practice of love. It's in work, in the rigorous exercise of powers of mind or body or spirit. It's a gift the created world is perpetually offering; the price of it is untiring attention to the present moment. It is to be found always and only in the contemplation of reality.

Hunt it down, pursue it, track it to its lair where it dwells. Not in pleasures and pastimes, distractions, piled-up satisfactions, and busyness. It dwells in truth, and nowhere else.

That's why it matters. It will show you moment by moment where truth is for you. And when you know that, cleave to it, turn not aside, be given up to that. That, if you will, is a way of life worth living.

But I haven't really said what I wanted to. There's more than that to joy. Hidden in its glowing heart, light beyond light. . . . How my blind eyes search the dazzling darkness to find out Him whom I have loved, whom I have sought, whom I have always desired.

THE VIRTUE OF POVERTY

All things were made by Him, and without Him
                    was not anything made that was made.
Here, I think, is the heart of the virtue of poverty. The stripping of the self implies it, of course, and is needed, but this is never more than a means. Poverty (a means, too) is near the End—it brings us very near.

The simple, enormous fact that every particle of matter was called into being—called by name, itself, alone—through the Word of God, constitutes an absolute demand for the practice of poverty. If our minds and senses are alive to the trace of God in all His creatures, we shall never waste nor spoil nor break. If we take and eat one piece of bread, how can we drop it half eaten and reach for another? If a length of cotton—grown from so miraculous a seed in so complex a soil, tended and harvested and woven and shaped by so many hands and minds; product in every atom of God our Father and, through Him, of man our brother—if such a scrap of stuff wears thin, shall we not hold it in careful hands? If it tears, shall we not mend it with love?

If we know—with what wonder!—that all things are various, particular, strange, and if we honor in them His work Who made them, we'll have to use them sparingly. Honoring Bach the maker and Shakespeare the maker, we honor God the Maker, Poet of heaven and earth and of all things visible and invisible. It follows that we won't listen to a fugue and read a sonnet at the same time, disfiguring the image of each with a careless half-attention.

Satiety, haste, boredom, restlessness, indifference, inattention, carelessness—all these are disorder of the soul, and poverty is health. In poverty we hunger and are filled, in the sweet order of God Who makes all things new. In poverty we make a deep and joyful reverence to the riches of creation. In poverty we answer with reflected love the potent, generating Love of God.

Because of this, St. Francis sang.

ATTENTION

I don't know much about music, but I know what I like.

Why can't I say even that much about people? The attention I pay to the Brahms *Violin Concerto* far surpasses in quality what I give to any human being whomsoever, friend or foe. The *Concerto* is easier, true. But a certain real effort is required, and I do make it—not always, but fairly often.

I settle myself quietly, empty myself of all extraneous thoughts, impressions, emotions, withdraw my attention from all outside sights, sounds, and concepts; and I listen. I turn my whole self to the music like radar; I become a receiver, percipient, minutely alive. I follow in busy quietude the shape of the music as its structure builds in my mind. I say nothing about it to myself, I am for this little space of time a pure act of listening.

I am not simple enough to be very good at this, nor do I have the musical education to hear all there is to be heard. But each time I listen I hear more, and more acutely.

This is surely the clue to the kind of attention I owe to people. I must empty my mind of other claims and, in interior silence, let them tell me who they are. I must remain in watchful, active quiet as the basic architecture of a personality presents itself to my mind. I must learn to hear a slight variation on a theme, a modulation to another key, an inner melody, a discord, an individual beauty of tone.

If love isn't this, it can't be much.

But the minute the note of another human being begins to sound, my self leaps up in clamant alarm and yells: "What about *me*! I'm here *too*!" In the ensuing din, I can't hear a thing.

I have a great deal to learn about the virtue of silence. I wish I could be quiet long enough to figure out how to begin.

COME AND SEE

In the beginning, the disciples came to Him and asked, "Where dwellest Thou?" And He answered: "Come and see." Come and see God, come and see Life.

Near the end, when they told Him Lazarus was dead, He asked, "Where have ye laid him?" And they answered: "Come and see." Man said to God, Come and see death. Come and see desolation, emptiness, cancellation. Come and see nothing.

Jesus wept.

But He came. He came, like Lazarus, to the grave. Bound hand and foot with graveclothes, a napkin bound about His face, He came to the tomb in the cave with a stone rolled against the door.

One day in Epiphany, reading the words, "Behold, the glory of the Lord is risen upon thee," I had a sudden sharp vision of Christ on the Cross—not graciously and symmetrically disposed there as in the usual crucifix, and not in a dramatic agony like a Grunewald. Just dead, plain dead. Battered, torn, bruised, drained, empty and gone. Dead as a mouse left on the doorstep by the family cat.

From such a nadir the sun of glory rose.

But no, that isn't it. That *was* the glory. Dead or alive, in His birth or in His death, He is all the glory that ever was, or is, or will be, for us. All our emptiness, and desolation, and cancellation, all our nothing, all our thousand deaths of heart and mind and spirit and body, He came to, He saw, He entered into, He took to Himself. And behold, they are risen with Him.

He descended into our Hell. And now the Light shines in the very deeps of our darkness, and no darkness can ever be deep enough to put it out.

Set at The Castle Press in Linotype Aldus,
a roman with old-face characteristics,
designed by Hermann Zapf.
Aldus was named for the 16th-century
Venetian printer Aldus Manutius.
Printed on Hallmark Eggshell Book paper.